FROM THE BIBLE-TEACHING MINISTRY OF
CHARLES R. SWINDOLL

D1567817

THE
Wise *Wild*
AND THE

30 DEVOTIONS ON WOMEN OF THE BIBLE

INSIGHT FOR LIVING

THE WISE AND THE WILD
30 Devotions on Women of the Bible
From the Bible-Teaching Ministry of Charles R. Swindoll

Charles R. Swindoll has devoted his life to the clear, practical teaching and application of God's Word and His grace. A pastor at heart, Chuck has served as senior pastor to congregations in Texas, Massachusetts, and California. He currently pastors Stonebriar Community Church in Frisco, Texas, but Chuck's listening audience extends far beyond a local church body. As a leading program in Christian broadcasting, *Insight for Living* airs in major Christian radio markets around the world, reaching people groups in languages they can understand. Chuck's extensive writing ministry has also served the body of Christ worldwide and his leadership as president and now chancellor of Dallas Theological Seminary has helped prepare and equip a new generation for ministry. Chuck and Cynthia, his partner in life and ministry, have four grown children and ten grandchildren.

Copyright © 2010 by Insight for Living.

All rights reserved worldwide under international copyright conventions. No portion of *The Wise and the Wild* may be reproduced, stored in a retrieval system, or transmitted in any form or by any means—electronic, mechanical, photocopy, recording, or any other—except for brief quotations in printed reviews, without the prior written permission of the publisher. Inquiries should be addressed to Insight for Living, Rights and Permissions, Post Office Box 251007, Plano, Texas, 75025-1007 or sent by e-mail to rights@insight.org.

Published By:
IFL Publishing House
A Division of Insight for Living
Post Office Box 251007
Plano, Texas 75025-1007

Editor in Chief: Cynthia Swindoll, President, Insight for Living
Executive Vice President: Wayne Stiles, Th.M., D.Min., Dallas Theological Seminary
Writers: Charles R. Swindoll, C.Th., Dallas Theological Seminary, D.D., L.H.D., LL.D., Litt.D.
John Adair, Th.M., Ph.D., Dallas Theological Seminary
Derrick G. Jeter, Th.M., Dallas Theological Seminary
Barb Peil, M.A., Christian Education, Dallas Theological Seminary
Wayne Stiles, Th.M., D.Min., Dallas Theological Seminary
Theological Editors: John Adair, Th.M., Ph.D., Dallas Theological Seminary
Derrick G. Jeter, Th.M., Dallas Theological Seminary
Wayne Stiles, Th.M., D.Min., Dallas Theological Seminary
Content Editor: Barb Peil, M.A., Christian Education, Dallas Theological Seminary
Copy Editors: Jim Craft, M.A., English, Mississippi College
Kathryn Merritt, M.A., English, Hardin-Simmons University
Project Coordinator, Creative Ministries: Melanie Munnell, M.A., Humanities,
The University of Texas at Dallas
Project Coordinator, Communications: Sarah Magnoni, A.A.S., University of Wisconsin
Proofreader: Paula Kyle, B.A., English, Texas A&M University-Commerce
Cover Designer: Margaret Gulliford, B.A., Graphic Design, Taylor University
Production Artist: Nancy Gustine, B.F.A., Advertising Art, University of North Texas

Unless otherwise identified, Scripture quotations are from the *New American Standard Bible*® (NASB). Copyright © 1960, 1962, 1963, 1968, 1971, 1972, 1973, 1975, 1977, 1995 by The Lockman Foundation, La Habra, California. All rights reserved. Used by permission. (www.lockman.org)

Scripture quotations marked (NIV) are taken from the *Holy Bible, New International Version*®. *NIV*®. Copyright © 1973, 1978, 1984 by International Bible Society. All rights reserved. Used by permission of Zondervan.

Quotations marked (NET) are from the *NET Bible*®. Copyright © 1996–2006 by Biblical Studies Press, L.L.C. (www.bible.org) All rights reserved. Scripture quoted by permission.

Scripture quotations marked (KJV) are from the *King James Version* of the Bible.

An effort has been made to locate sources and obtain permission where necessary for the quotations used in this Bible Companion. In the event of any unintentional omission, a modification will gladly be incorporated in future printings.

ISBN: 978-1-57972-882-3
Printed in the United States of America

Table of Contents

A Word to Wise
and Wonderful Women

A Note from Chuck Swindoll

It is no secret that God has blessed my life by surrounding me with amazing women. I'm convinced they have been tools that God has used to strengthen *and* soften this man.

Allow me to introduce my VIPs:

My beloved wife of fifty-four years, Cynthia, whose commitment knows no bounds and who encourages me beyond measure. Our mutual partnership throughout our lifetime of ministry together has been a source of immeasurable joy and love. Cynthia's influence on my life has been multifaceted. First, I've never known a day when she didn't love Christ. You can't say that about many people. I've never known her love for Him to cool or to become inconsistent. She has never grown weary in her walk with Christ. Also, her affectionate support of me personally and her own commitment to excellence in leading Insight for Living for more than three decades has kept me faithful to my own calling "in season and out of season."

As I think of my mother, Lovell, two words come to mind: *class* and *zest*. My mother, being a "classy woman," was determined to keep our family from being ignorant of the arts or lacking in social graces. I have her to thank for my love of artistic beauty and fine music as well as my knowledge of which fork to use and how to avoid getting gravy on my tie. She also possessed a tireless zest for life. I am indebted to her for endowing me with enthusiasm and relentless drive. Her indomitable spirit got passed on to all three of us kids, thank goodness.

I learned to love life from my sister, Luci. For as long as I can remember, her influence on me has been positive, specifically in the areas of my developing a sense of humor, having joy in life, and looking at the glass half-full rather than half-empty. She is the only one I allow to call me "Babe." She's my beloved sister . . . faithful and loyal to the end and always ready with a word of encouragement, a funny story, or a strong affirmation. That's Luci, and that's been true of her all my years.

My life is full of charming beauty . . . in character, face, and heart . . . thanks to our two daughters Charissa and Colleen and two daughters-in-law Debbie and Jeni. Each one deserves my enormous respect and love.

Through these women and a handful of other gifted, wise women friends and partners in ministry, I have seen modeled the critical difference a godly character makes. Complementing that picture is the unique blend of color from their feminine paintbrush.

A woman's character has a beautiful way of affecting an ever-widening circle of influence. Let's face it, men are listening to women more today than they ever have. If I had my way, we certainly would! I've seen women under duress and pressure emerge with real strength and dignity, causing second and third looks from the men in their lives.

We would be wise to look once or twice again at the realistic portraits of women that Scripture paints. God gives us living portraits in colors true to their characters—some dark, others bright, some wise, others wild—all of them at crossroads of choice, confronting their culture and times.

Such is the timeless call of faith.

In this little book, we've gathered together a collection of portraits, really just snapshots, of thirty women of the Bible. We've pictured them in a realistic light, so that we might learn well the variety of lessons from their lives. Even the wicked ones have helpful things to teach us. And the godly ones inspire us to deeper trust in our good and faithful God.

Our goal, of course, is to encourage you to walk with God all the days of your life, to be a woman who takes God seriously. Now, that has nothing to do with your skills, your giftedness, or how you're wired. You'll see in our gallery that these women come from all corners of life, but they have one thing in common: they are each confronted with a choice of how they will walk before God—in reverence or in defiance, in submission or in pride.

Their choices are not all that different from the choices that you live with every day. I'm a realist enough to know that all of you, married or single, young or seasoned, need help in knowing how to navigate the choppy waters of normal life.

You need some directions from God, from His Word, if on nothing more than just how to cope, how to hold on, how to deal with the pressures of merging life with godliness.

We're praying that the lessons from these women's lives will add a godly momentum in this journey you're already on, that in the fear of the Lord you will find a growing stability. In this greater reverence for God, you'll discover how the Spirit comes to your assistance, calms your heart, and points your feet in the right direction. We pray that you'll find here in this book helpful touches of insight and enormous comfort in knowing how to walk with the Lord.

And for the men who are sneaking a peek at this devotional about women, good for you! Learn all you can from these women whom God gave us as warnings and examples. Honor the godly women He's put in your life as fellow heirs of the grace of life (1 Peter 3:7).

I know the more time I spend on this earth, the more thankful I grow for the beautiful partnership that men and women share and the nuances of godliness they uniquely model.

Chuck Swindoll

Charles R. Swindoll

THE
Wise
AND THE *Wild*

30 DEVOTIONS ON WOMEN OF THE BIBLE

For whatever was written in earlier times was written for our instruction, so that through perseverance and the encouragement of the Scriptures we might have hope.

—Romans 15:4

They heard the sound of the LORD God walking in the garden in the cool of the day, and the man and his wife hid themselves from the presence of the LORD God among the trees of the garden.

—Genesis 3:8

Eve
LIVING WITH CONSEQUENCES

Once upon a time they had been happy. Love at first sight, some called it.

Embossed in Eve's memory was the way Adam had looked at her that first time. He held her close and whispered in her ear, "I found you!"

And now she can't find him—only the shadow of the man she once knew. He's distant, distracted, caught up in a dream of a far-off place.

She remembered that place too. A paradise. Love came easily to them there. With God as their witness, they pledged their love. But their time in the garden was only a honeymoon—a brief, joyful interruption of life—an escape at best. Living east of Eden now, she had come to accept that *this* was their life. They had chosen this road. There was no escaping the consequences of their choice to experience life apart from God.

At night from their front steps they could see the glow from the flaming sword and cherubim that God had placed to guard the entrance to the garden. They had once been king and queen of that tropical paradise; now it was forbidden land.

All this because of one choice that changed everything.

The decades-old question taunted Eve's mind. *What if? What if? What if?* What if she had seen through the Enemy's deception? What if Adam had stood his ground? What if they had taken the way of escape from this temptation? What if they had chosen God's plan instead of theirs? God told them not to eat of the tree of the knowledge of good and evil, yet in spite of His warning, Eve did what *she* thought best . . . and Adam followed. And immediately they felt the consequences.

In one tragic moment, Eve stood alone before God, guilty and without excuse. Gone were the days of walking with Him in the cool of the day. Now she could hardly remember the sound of His voice—except for the tone of it when she ran from Him in fear. As for her relationship with Adam . . . that was broken into ten different pieces.

The choice to sin will do that. Sin divides. Sin destroys. Every time.

It would take a plan only God could put in motion to redeem Eve's relationships and restore this beautiful, tragic scene.

—*Barb Peil*

The Rest of the Story: Read Genesis 3.

Take It to *Heart*

Every day you will be tempted with the sin of choosing your way over God's way. Do you take God seriously? Are you in any way rationalizing a "small sin" to satisfy your wishes and wants? To get what *you* think you need? To do and communicate what *you* think is best? Ask the Lord to show you the way of escape from this sin that will surely destroy. Consider the lesson from Eve's life and ponder 1 Corinthians 10:13. Seek the Lord for the way of escape from your personal struggle. Capture your thoughts, prayers, or commitments in the space below.

Then [Hagar] called the name of the LORD who spoke to her, "You are a God who sees."

—Genesis 16:13

Hagar
Meeting God on the Run

God had promised an heir to Abram . . . and yet God prevented conception. Go figure.

This tension eventually proved too much for Abram's wife, Sarai. It seemed the only thing worse than the barren land she lived in was the barren womb she bore. So Sarai pointed to Hagar, her Egyptian maid, and told Abram to provide a child through her. The culture allowed for this custom, but it was never God's plan.

After Hagar conceived, she despised Sarai, who then became resentful and mistreated her maid. Not surprisingly, Hagar fled. The plan backfired.

The Lord found Hagar "by a spring of water in the wilderness, by the spring on the way to Shur" (Genesis 16:7). The location of the spring reveals that Hagar intended to head back home—to Egypt. But God told the expectant mother to return to Sarai and to name the baby *Ishmael*—meaning, "God hears"—with the explanation, "for the LORD has heard of your misery" (16:11 NIV). Hagar called the Lord *El Roi*, "the God who sees me" (16:13 NIV). She named the spring by which she sat *Beer Lahai Roi*, which could be rendered, "the well of the Living One who sees me." (See 16:13–14.)

Abram had run to Egypt to escape a famine (Genesis 12:10–20), Sarai had turned to an Egyptian maid to escape barrenness, and Hagar had run to Egypt to escape misery. But every plan of escape, apart from the will of God, found each person back at the same place of having to trust the Lord all over again.

Hagar's obedient return to a miserable and tough situation reveals her faith in the God who met her on the run. The meanings of the names "God hears" and "God sees" remain as constant reminders of how best to respond in desperate times.

In times of seemingly inescapable despair, the Lord wants His children to turn to Him rather than "run to Egypt." As we wait on the Lord, we cling to His promise that He waits with us and will provide for us, for *God hears* our prayers and *God sees* our needs. Those names become God's promises to us . . . and our reasons for trusting Him, even when circumstances offer no rational hope for relief.

— Wayne Stiles

*A careful reader will notice that Abram's and Sarai's names later changed to Abraham and Sarah (Genesis 17:5, 15). This was a practical way God showed that their hearts had been changed by His grace.

The Rest of the Story: Read Genesis 16:1–16.

Take It to *Heart*

Are you traveling the road to Shur today, running from a difficult situation—and running away from an opportunity to trust God? How does the fact that "God sees" you in your trial and "God hears" your cry change the way you feel today? How does this truth about God's character stir faith in you to trust Him more? Write down your conversation with the Lord here.

And the LORD said to Abraham, "Why did Sarah laugh, saying, 'Shall I indeed bear a child, when I am so old?' Is anything too difficult for the LORD? At the appointed time I will return to you, at this time next year, and Sarah will have a son."

—Genesis 18:13–14

Sarah
LEARNING TO LAUGH AT LIFE'S IMPOSSIBILITIES

She had never heard anything so preposterous in her life, and her 89-year-old ears had heard plenty of ridiculous claims. When she was 65, her husband said God had commanded them to leave their home and head for who-knows-where. God had told him, so Abraham reported to her, that God would make them "a great nation" (Genesis 12:2) and give the land of Canaan as a perpetual inheritance to their descendants. *A great nation . . . descendants . . . that's a great joke!* she must have thought. They didn't have one child, much less a whole household of them. How could a nation come from a barren couple?

That's why Sarah, while standing at the tent flap and eavesdropping on the conversation of Abraham and three strangers, thought she had heard the most outlandish words ever spoken: "I will surely return to you at this time next year; and behold, Sarah your wife shall have a son" (18:10). In utter disbelief, she laughed to herself.

But God got the last laugh. Within a matter of months, 90-year-old Sarah was carrying a baby boy in her womb, and just as the Lord promised, she delivered her son to her 100-year-old husband. Abraham named the boy Isaac — which means "he laughs." And from that moment until their dying days, Isaac was a living reminder that God is the God of the outlandish — the God of the impossible. He is the one who can turn the laughter of doubt into the laughter of rejoicing.

When God announced the promised conception of Isaac, He asked, in response to Sarah's doubt, "Is anything too difficult for the LORD?" (Genesis 18:14). The Lord would answer His own question two thousand years later when He dispatched the angel Gabriel to announce another impossible birth to a young virgin girl: "Nothing will be impossible with God" (Luke 1:37).

We all face impossibilities in life, from a human perspective. But the God whom we worship is the God of impossibilities. All of us are on the journey of faith, struggling to believe that God is able to and will meet the needs of our impossibilities. So, when these impossibilities of life come, trust God — He just might make the impossible possible. And you just might fall down in faithful laughter because it was too preposterous to believe.

— *Derrick G. Jeter*

The Rest of the Story: Read Genesis 17:15–17; 18:9–15; 21:1–7.

Take It to *Heart*

Have you struggled with trusting God in the past? Explain.
What impossibility are you facing today? Are you believing
God to make your impossibility possible? Why, or why not?

_____

_____

_____

_____

_____

_____

_____

_____

_____

_____

_____

_____

_____

_____

_____

_____

_____

_____

_____

But [Lot's] wife, from behind him, looked back, and she became a pillar of salt.

—Genesis 19:26

Lot's Wife

She may not have said it out loud, but her backward glance said it all. She didn't want to leave.

For some strange reason, Lot and his wife were drawn to Sodom. They had lived among openly indecent, perverted people and had tolerated them, then became accustomed to them, and finally were accepting of their ways.

Then God stepped in. Jealous for Lot's deliverance, God clearly announced an evacuation plan from the approaching doomsday: "Escape for your life! Do not look behind you, and do not stay anywhere in the valley; escape to the mountains, or you will be swept away" (Genesis 19:17). No complicated riddles, just three shouts:

Run! Don't look back! Don't stop!

But Lot's wife lingered. And even though she had heard as clearly as Lot had, she turned around anyway—not out of curiosity but out of longing. She refused to cut her emotional ties. *All this business of running away and not looking back is awfully extreme. God couldn't have meant what He said.* She didn't take God seriously, so she looked.

In a second, God made her an object lesson.

Lot and his girls didn't even know she was missing until they arrived at their destination. Perhaps they came back later and saw the pillar of salt that had been their wife and mother. How eerie!

Even in the face of destruction, a person who is caught in a destructive lifestyle will continue it. How else can you explain why people stay on drugs when they know it's killing them? Or continue in immorality, knowing it's destroying those they love? There's something about the sin that's greater than logic.

God finally got fed up with it. Behind His warning to Lot's family, the worst holocaust in ancient civilization was unfolding: "Then the Lord rained on Sodom and Gomorrah brimstone and fire" (Genesis 19:24). Lot and his daughters probably felt the heat on their backs as the corrupt cities were incinerated and sank slowly into the ground and the waters of the Dead Sea washed and bubbled over the destruction.

Here's our warning: if, by the grace of God, you choose to leave a wrong lifestyle, don't look back. You will only hinder the recovery process. Something disastrous occurs in us when we intentionally remember the pleasurable sin that was ruining us. That second glance makes us grow weak.

Call it naive, call it simplistic, call it whatever you want, but whatever you do, don't look back.

— *Charles R. Swindoll*

The Rest of the Story: Read Genesis 19:15–26.

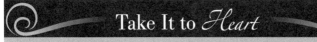

Take It to *Heart*

What is the specific sin in your past that you must not ever look back on? Are you taking God's warning seriously?

_____

_____

_____

_____

_____

_____

_____

_____

_____

_____

_____

_____

_____

_____

_____

_____

_____

_____

_____

_____

Then Miriam and Aaron spoke against Moses because of the Cushite woman whom he had married . . . and they said, "Has the LORD indeed spoken only through Moses? Has He not spoken through us as well?" And the LORD heard it.

—Numbers 12:1–2

Miriam
OVERCOMING A PRIDEFUL SPIRIT

Miriam occupied a privileged place in the "first family" of Israel alongside her younger brothers Moses and Aaron. Despite her impressive pedigree and her faithfulness to the Lord, a lengthy and seemingly aimless wandering in the wilderness, the constant complaints of her people, and even the recent loss of many lives in God's judgment created a situation where Miriam was ripe for failure.

Upset over Moses's decision to marry a non-Israelite woman, Miriam publicly questioned his leadership. Surely, Miriam thought, *she* was at least as qualified to lead the Israelites as Moses was. Caught up in her pride and presumption, Miriam forgot to account for one thing: God was listening. She was so focused on what she thought was best that she ended up undermining the authority not just of Moses but of God, the One who gave Moses his position of leadership.

God, in turn, reminded Miriam and Aaron of their identity—prophets who saw God revealed in visions and dreams—in contrast to Moses's identity—one who spoke with the Lord face-to-face. God judged Miriam with a brief bout of leprosy for attempting to denigrate His unique relationship with Moses and to usurp Moses's God-given authority. She was banished from her people for a week while participating in the cleansing rituals prescribed by the Law of Moses.

Miriam's circumstance reveals what for many well-meaning Christians can be a subtle sin: pride. Up to that point, Miriam had lived her life as a faithful follower of God. In that, her life mirrors many of our own lives: we try to follow God faithfully, we pray and read our Bibles regularly, and we attend church and serve His people on a regular basis. But there come times, even for faithful believers, when in our pride we're tempted to think we know or can do better than our leaders.

We need to be on guard against this subtle sin of thinking too highly of ourselves based on our past track record. Before long, we'll likely find ourselves in Miriam's position, tempted to undermine our leaders or to think we know better than God does. Let's take our cue from Moses instead of Miriam and strive to live lives more humble "than any man who was on the face of the earth" (Numbers 12:3).

—John Adair

The Rest of the Story: Read Numbers 12:1–15.

Take It to *Heart*

Consider an area in your life that stirs in you a critical spirit. Ask yourself, "How might I be working to undermine someone's God-given authority in my life? Am I thinking too much or too often of myself? Is the Lord trying to reveal to me my pride?"

_____

_____

_____

_____

_____

_____

_____

_____

_____

_____

_____

_____

_____

_____

_____

_____

_____

So the men said to [Rahab], "Our life for yours if you do not tell this business of ours; and it shall come about when the LORD gives us the land that we will deal kindly and faithfully with you."

— Joshua 2:14

Rahab
Demonstrating Courageous Faith

She had a reputation no woman would ever want: she was a harlot, a prostitute. But she was also a woman whose courage and faith in God would transcend her reputation and place her in the lineage of the Messiah.

Rahab owned a house, built on the outer walls of Jericho. When two Israelite spies came to town, Rahab turned the roof of her house into a hiding place for them — an act which took courage. The people of Jericho were terrified because they had heard of all the miraculous things God had done for His people after their escape from Egypt. When commanded by the rulers of the city to turn the men over, Rahab concealed their identities and whereabouts — an act of faith in God.

Rahab had come to believe in the spies' God: "The Lord your God, He is God in heaven above and on earth beneath" (Joshua 2:11). Knowing the Israelites would conquer the land, Rahab asked the spies to spare her life and the lives of her family members when the assault came. The spies agreed to do so if she would keep their secret, place her family safely inside her house, and tie a scarlet ribbon in her window as a signal to the Israelite army to spare her home.

Later, when Joshua and the army appeared and attacked the city, only Rahab and her family survived.

For her courageous faith, this woman with a bad reputation was enrolled among the faithful in the book of Hebrews—the only woman, besides Sarah, named there (Hebrews 11:31). James used Rahab as an example of how a character can be transformed by a living faith that yields works (James 2:25). And eventually, she was no longer known as the harlot who hid the spies but as the wife of Salmon, the mother of Boaz, and the ancestor of Jesus (Matthew 1:5–16).

If you have a past you're not proud of, don't despair. God's grace is sufficient to transform a bad reputation into a sterling one. All that is required is faith—faith in the One, Jesus Christ, who came through the lineage of a harlot. And when someone reminds you of your past, courageously stand and declare: "What I once was, I am not now. I am a new person, for the One who died once for me has given me a new name— daughter of the Messiah." (See Romans 6:10; 2 Corinthians 5:17; Revelation 2:17.)

—*Derrick G. Jeter*

The Rest of the Story: Read Joshua 2:1–21.

Take It to *Heart*

What is the difference between your old reputation before Christ and your new reputation in Christ? What strengths (such as an increased gratitude for forgiveness, a compassion for those struggling, and so on) do you now have because you have been redeemed from your sinful past?

Deborah said to Barak, "Arise! For this is the day in which the LORD has given Sisera into your hands; behold, the LORD has gone out before you."

—Judges 4:14

Deborah
LEADING IN A TIME OF CHAOS

Meet Deborah: a strong, capable leader in a chaotic man's world. She called herself "a mother in Israel" (Judges 5:7). Maintaining her heart for her family, Deborah also believed there was more in her life than just working in the home. With an ear for God's voice, Deborah rose to a place of authority in the land during a time of great instability. There was no king; there were no laws — "every man did what was right in his own eyes" (17:6).

But in every generation, God raises up men and women to stand for Him and defend His purposes. In this period of the judges, Deborah spoke for God, and people came to her for wisdom. Like an ancient Golda Meir, Deborah was also the go-to woman for Israel's strategic defense. And being of such a stripe, she rose to prominence when a war broke out.

Outnumbered and out-rigged against Canaanite forces that had terrorized Israel for a generation, Deborah rallied Israel's rag-tag army. She called out Barak, Israel's top general who had shrunken back from the enemy's intimidation. Rather than shame him for his lack of faith or usurp him when he failed to lead, she charged him to be God's warrior and lead Israel into battle. Per his request, she went with him to the battlefield, and when it came time for the attack, she was his best cheerleader. With enthusiasm and faith, she turned his focus from the

Canaanite arsenal of nine hundred iron chariots to the mighty arm of God. And in a crazy "quirk" of weather—the battle-field flooded and the chariots got stuck in the mud—Israel prevailed.

Barak had Deborah to thank when his name showed up in the "Hall of Faith" of Hebrews 11, as he "gained strength in weakness [and] became mighty in battle" (Hebrews 11:34 NET).

In perfect harmony, Deborah and Barak's roles comple-mented each other to achieve an impossible victory; they were two bright lights in a dark sky. And as the credits rolled on the close of this story, the Israelites heard Deborah and Barak sing-ing a duet—a song of deliverance celebrating God's victory.

—Barb Peil

The Rest of the Story: Read Judges 4–5.

Take It to *Heart*

Where are your areas of influence? Are you embracing your God-given role to further His purposes? Consider how your influence inspires others, especially those who are fearful or not living up to God's call on their lives. Make a list here of areas where you can instill courage into those who need your encouragement of faith. Ask the Lord to use you to help those in your life gain strength in weakness and be mighty in battle! Speak a good word today to someone who is faltering.

[Samson] loved a woman in the valley of Sorek, whose name was Delilah.

Delilah
Tempting a Man to Death

The lips of an adulteress drip honey / And smoother than oil is her speech" (Proverbs 5:3). How true of a woman who uses her feminine charm to beguile and deceive morally weak men to fall into sin.

Delilah was one such woman. And Samson was one such man.

Delilah made her home in the valley of Sorek; a valley Samson knew well. At one end was the Philistine town of Timnah, where he had fallen in love with a Philistine woman (Judges 14:1–2). At the other end was Zorah, the hometown of Samson's father (13:2).

It was there, in the valley of Sorek, that the rulers of the Philistines bribed Delilah to entice Samson into her bedroom to discover the secret of his strength. Samson was physically strong but morally weak and an easy conquest for Delilah. On three separate occasions, as Samson enjoyed himself at Delilah's home, she pressed him to tell her his secret. Toying with her, Samson told Delilah that seven fresh bowstrings or brand new ropes or the locks of his hair woven into a loom would sap his strength—but none did. Yet the cunning Delilah soon discovered his real weakness—illustrating the powerful charms of a deceptive and persistent woman. The secret was in his long and beautiful hair—grown since birth in observance of Samson's Nazirite vow never to cut it (Judges 13:5).

Lulling Samson to sleep in her lap, Delilah alerted the Philistine rulers who waited in the shadows to capture him. They sheared Samson's hair and, in his newly weakened state, bound him, gouged out his eyes, and forced him to grind grain in the prison at Gaza.

And Delilah? She simply walked off the pages of history.

Delilah knew that her body could be used as a weapon. Preying on weak men or even strong men in weak moments, women can use the visual advantage to manipulate and control. When a woman uses her body as a tool, trouble is soon to follow.

—*Derrick G. Jeter*

The Rest of the Story: Read Judges 16:4–21.

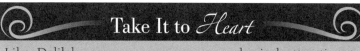

Take It to Heart

Like Delilah, some women can use physical attraction to gain ungodly advantage. Truth be told, every woman has the power to tempt the opposite sex. You decide every day to be modest or manipulative in your choices of dress, speech, and eye contact. How can you guard yourself from the ungodly desire to control?

"Do not urge me to leave you or turn back from following you; for where you go, I will go, and where you lodge, I will lodge. Your people shall be my people, and your God, my God."

—Ruth 1:16

Ruth

Finding God's Grace in Life's Hurts

Life hurts.

No matter what century you live in, there are times when circumstances unfold in ways you hope they never will. People die. Crises strike. Hopes are crushed. And when the smoke clears, you feel alone. Wounded and alone.

That's the way Naomi felt: far from home, a widow, and a mother to two sons recently laid in their graves. The only joy in her life was her young daughter-in-law, Ruth. Also a widow. Also desperate in a world harsh to women who were alone.

Picture the scene. Two women walk in the undulating heat across the wilderness. One old and shattered. One young and heartbroken. One heading home to Bethlehem. One leaving home in Moab. One in kindness bidding her young daughter-in-law to stay behind. One in kindness committing her loyalty to stay with.

Neither woman could have dreamed the illustration God was making of their lives nor could they have imaged God's provision that waited on the other side of the desert. They had only the Lord to provide for them, and He had the details of their rescue already in place.

35

For Naomi, rescue meant food and water and shelter. It meant a loving family and friends. Naomi needed healing. She came back to her hometown broken and bitter, saying, "I went out full, but the LORD has brought me back empty" (Ruth 1:21).

For Ruth, rescue meant eternally more. What seemed like a tragedy in this young widow's life was in reality a step on the path that led her to faith in God.

At no point in all the trials that Ruth encountered did she resist or become hardened. Her heart remained open, though broken. She embraced Naomi's lead in returning to Bethlehem and then followed her advice on how to fit into this new culture, even on how to capture the attention of Boaz, who would become her kinsman-redeemer.

This true story ended happier than anyone could have guessed. Ruth's marriage to Boaz, a romantic tale in itself, made the record books. Their son Obed (the sparkle in his grand-mother Naomi's eyes) became the grandfather of the great King David, the line into which Jesus Christ was born.

Who would have guessed that in a time that seemed dark-est for Ruth, God's grace would show up the brightest? When her life hurt the most, He redeemed her loss and provided not only for her immediate need but for her salvation . . . as well as an honored place in the lineage of the Savior of the world.

— Barb Peil

The Rest of the Story: Read the book of Ruth.

Take It to *Heart*

Can you imagine now the illustration God is making from the current scene of your life? He sees the difficult details you face today. He is using whatever crisis you may be enduring to bring about His good purposes in and through your life. Today is not the end. What need will you entrust to Him to meet today?

_____

_____

_____

_____

_____

_____

_____

_____

_____

_____

_____

_____

_____

_____

She made a vow and said, "O LORD of hosts, if You will indeed look on the affliction of Your maidservant and remember me, and not forget Your maidservant, but will give Your maidservant a son, then I will give him to the LORD all the days of his life."

— 1 Samuel 1:11

Hannah
RELEASING THE CHILD GOD GAVE

The fifteen-mile journey from Ramah to Shiloh took merely a day to travel. But for Hannah, it must have felt like weeks.

Her husband's other wife jabbered incessantly to her sons and daughters, always loud enough for Hannah to hear. The snobbery added weight to Hannah's silent burden. Her empty arms ached for a son. And because the other wife had children, Hannah's problem was obvious to all: God had closed her womb.

She looked at the road beneath her sandals. Centuries earlier, this well-worn path had known the likes of the patriarchs Abraham, Isaac, and Jacob — all who had barren wives as well. The thought of their miraculous conceptions may have roused hope in Hannah's heart. Shiloh was just ahead where she would worship. Hannah determined to ask God for a son.

She made her way to the tabernacle where behind several curtains glowed the holy presence of God. Approaching the doorway, she fashioned the words in her mind. As tears warmed her face, she made her request (1 Samuel 1:11).

After Hannah and her husband returned to Ramah, God gave her a son — Samuel. Once he was weaned, Hannah journeyed again to Shiloh to give Samuel back to God — just as she had promised in her prayer to the Lord. Placing her boy in the care of the priest Eli, Hannah returned home again with empty arms.

Even though Hannah would see Samuel each year at the feasts, it would have been heartrending to leave the son she had cared for every day for three years. And yet, she knew from the beginning the day would come, for she had vowed to give her son to God's service. Samuel was not hers to keep. In reality, no child is.

Hannah's release of Samuel reveals the attitude all godly parents should adopt. God gives us children so that we may give them back to Him. Sons and daughters are like arrows to be aimed . . . and then released (Psalm 127:3–5).

In surrendering a child to God's purposes, the humble parent bows not in an admission of defeat but, like Hannah, in an act of worship.

—*Wayne Stiles*

The Rest of the Story: Read 1 Samuel 1:1–28.

If you are a parent, most likely you understand the struggle of releasing your children to God. Because circumstances are out of your control, you most certainly will be forced to entrust their health, their choices, and their futures to God. Have you been asked to do that yet? If not, what can you do now to prepare yourself for when your heart is put to the test? If so, how can you encourage another parent who is now in that difficult process?

In the heart of every believer who is surrendered to God, there lies the tension of loving your most precious "something" and also having to place that "something" into His hands. What have you learned about the character of God that makes this personal surrender possible?

Then David said to Abigail, "Blessed be the LORD God of Israel, who sent you this day to meet me, and blessed be your discernment, and blessed be you, who have kept me this day from bloodshed and from avenging myself by my own hand."

— 1 Samuel 25:32 – 33

Abigail
SAVING HER HUSBAND'S NECK

If he is honest, almost every husband has a story about how his wife rescued him . . . usually from himself. (I have several!) By her wisdom and tact, a godly wife keeps her husband from doing or saying something that he would later regret.

Abigail saved her husband Nabal's neck—I mean that, literally. She rescued him from a violent death, a peril he brought upon himself by his own foolishness. First Samuel 25 unfolds an account of passion, danger, irony, and intrigue—like a story out of a classic Western movie with wide-open country, gritty heroes on horses, a tough and beautiful heroine, and a hard-hearted villain who complicates life for everyone. Only this story isn't fiction, and it revolves around three complex, conflicted characters who are on a collision course.

The gritty heroes were David—before he was king—and a couple hundred loyal, hardworking, rugged men who protected local ranchers' livestock from thieves and wild animals. They were self-appointed police who provided a service, usually to grateful ranchers.

The villain was a man named Nabal, whose name appropriately means "foolish" and who refused to pay the normal "gratuity" to David and his men. In spite of the fact that Nabal was wealthy, he put himself in harm's way because of his stubborn, stupid, tightwad decision.

Nabal's impudent response brought out the worst in David. The future king wasn't yet the mature man of God that he would become. So with the pounding of war beating in his chest, David headed for Nabal's house . . . out for blood.

These two men were vulnerable at their worst moments.

Enter: the heroine. Abigail was as intelligent and beautiful as her husband was harsh and dishonest. The irony is painful. How could a woman having such obvious wisdom be married to a loser named Fool? This was a dreadful marriage, probably arranged. As a result, Abigail suffered . . . but the casual observer wouldn't know it to see her.

If she had been cunning, Abigail might have thought, *Oh, my. David's on his way to kill old Fool? Well, God moves in mysterious ways, His wonders to perform!* But she didn't go there. She immediately put a plan in motion that protected her husband from harm, not because he deserved it, not because he was good, but because *she* was good. God was at work in the woman's heart. Despite how stupid a husband Nabal was, Abigail chose to remain honorable in her role as his partner.

By the way, the account ends with a wonderful twist. Nabal, so shocked when he discovered he had narrowly escaped David's wrath, dropped stone-cold dead. And the beautiful Abigail? David swept her off her feet as his new wife . . . and they rode away into the sunset.

—*Charles R. Swindoll*

The Rest of the Story: Read 1 Samuel 25. Read also 1 Peter 2:23 to see how Jesus handled injustice.

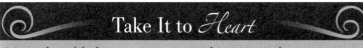

More than likely, you interact with some authority in your life who sometimes acts like Nabal. Review your actions and attitudes toward that person. Does your response reflect what he or she deserves, or do you act and think out of your choice of godly character? Ask the Lord to help you respond in a way that pleases Him.

_____

_____

_____

_____

_____

_____

_____

_____

_____

_____

_____

_____

_____

_____

_____

_____

Now when evening came David arose from his bed and walked around on the roof of the king's house, and from the roof he saw a woman bathing; and the woman was very beautiful in appearance. So David sent and inquired about the woman. And one said, "Is this not Bathsheba, the daughter of Eliam, the wife of Uriah the Hittite?"

—2 Samuel 11:2–3

Bathsheba
WALKING INTO ADULTERY

As the lively, warm afternoon sun of spring gave way to the still, cool dark of night, a beautiful woman stood on her roof-top and prepared to bathe. The water cascaded over her body while King David took a stroll on the roof of the king's palace some distance away. He caught sight of her, but instead of turning away and protecting his heart from temptation, he fixed his adulterous gaze on her. His desire for her swelled, and after confirming that he knew who she was—including that she was already married—David sent messengers to bring Bathsheba to the palace.

The Bible records no instance of protest on Bathsheba's part, either to the messengers who brought her to the palace or to the king who clearly intended to have her. After her illicit encounter with the king, Bathsheba washed herself again and returned home. Within a matter of weeks, she realized she was with child and, in a brief message, told David, "I am pregnant" (2 Samuel 11:5). Once David executed his plan to cover up the pregnancy—which included having Bathsheba's husband killed—she mourned her loss and quickly married the king before she delivered the child.

Bathsheba's role in the encounter with David has been notoriously difficult to interpret. Most of the questions surrounding this event ask whether or not she was bathing on her roof to tempt David, for she had to know that she was within sight of the palace. However, whether she was a crafty seductress or a naïve, newly married girl, Bathsheba's silence—rather than protest—stands out in the encounter. When the opportunity arose for her to resist, she did not.

And this is the real lesson of Bathsheba's fall into sin: we are all responsible for what we do. Whether we actively pursue a relationship outside of marriage or if we just let ourselves fall into one, we make choices. Choices were made by David and Bathsheba all along the way toward their adulterous encounter, and the same is true of anyone who falls into sexual sin today. We must be vigilant to protect our sexuality. Rather than simply avoiding sin, we must concern ourselves with pursuing purity. It's a choice we can't afford not to make.

—John Adair

The Rest of the Story: Read 2 Samuel 11:1–5, 26–27.

Examine your life. Is there anything that could compromise your moral, godly desires if a relationship with the opposite sex escalated to the next level? What can you do to avoid impurity and pursue righteousness (2 Timothy 2:22)?

_____

_____

_____

_____

_____

_____

_____

_____

_____

_____

_____

_____

_____

_____

_____

_____

Now when the queen of Sheba heard about the fame of Solomon concerning the name of the LORD, she came to test him with difficult questions. So she came to Jerusalem with a very large retinue, with camels carrying spices and very much gold and precious stones. When she came to Solomon, she spoke with him about all that was in her heart.

— 1 Kings 10:1–2

The Queen of Sheba

SEEKING TRUTH AND WISDOM

For days the desert was filled with the sweet aroma of spices, hanging heavy in the arid air and penetrating anything that passed through. With a southern breeze sweeping up the Jerusalem hillside, the sweetness of the spices may have filled Solomon's palace, announcing the arrival of the Queen of Sheba.

On camelback the Queen of the Sabeans traveled with her entourage twelve hundred miles from her home in southern Arabia to Israel's capital city. She made this arduous, though sweet-smelling, journey no doubt to establish a political and commercial alliance with the powerful kingdom of Israel, ruled by the renowned King Solomon. But as an intellectually curious woman, she also made the journey because she had heard of Solomon's wisdom and wealth, and she desired "to test him with difficult questions" (1 Kings 10:1).

After arriving in Jerusalem, the breathtaking splendor of Solomon's house, of his hospitality, and of his wisdom compelled the queen to praise Solomon's God and shower Solomon with extravagant gifts of gold, spices, stones, and almug trees. When she prepared to leave Jerusalem and make the journey to her homeland, Solomon presented gifts to her from his "royal bounty" (10:13). But she left with more than valuable trinkets;

she left with the priceless gift of wisdom—the one gift she desired above all others.

Wisdom is the one incalculable and irreplaceable commodity. When the Queen of Sheba came to Solomon's court, she was wise enough to seek additional wisdom from the wisest man of her day. She understood that the most valuable thing she could do for herself and her kingdom was to "buy truth, and . . . not sell it, / [to] Get wisdom and instruction and understanding" (Proverbs 23:23). The Queen paid a high price to seek truth and get wisdom, but she would have paid any price to satisfy her intellectual curiosity, her need to know truth. What personal price would you pay? How curious are you?

Solomon learned from his father and mother that he should:

> "Acquire wisdom;
> And with all your acquiring, get understanding.
> Prize her, and she will exalt you;
> She will honor you if you embrace her.
> She will place on your head a garland of grace;
> She will present you with a crown of beauty."
> (Proverbs 4:7–9)

Every woman who satisfies her intellectual curiosity by seeking wisdom from above and "buying" God's truth is a woman of grace and beauty. And if you do both, many will rise up and call you a woman of worth.

—Derrick G. Jeter

The Rest of the Story: Read 1 Kings 10:1–13.

Take It to *Heart*

How curious are you about God? Are there depths you'd still like to go in your relationship with Him, to better understand His ways? What stimulates your thinking? List here the best books you've read and what they've been about. What areas of curiosity would you like to explore more? What price are you willing to pay to satisfy your curiosity?

Do not be bound together with unbelievers; for what partnership have righteousness and lawlessness, or what fellowship has light with darkness?

—2 Corinthians 6:14

The Wives of Solomon

TURNING THE HEART OF A SPOUSE

Marriage has a tremendous influence on spiritual life.

When a believer marries an unbeliever, the believer must tolerate beliefs, habits, and passions that are contrary to the Bible. Eventually, that toleration can lead to spiritual compromise . . . or, worse, to spiritual collapse.

That's why God regularly warned His people against intermarriage with foreigners: "For they will turn your sons away from following Me" (Deuteronomy 7:4; see also Exodus 34:12–17). And because the kings of Israel would lead by example, the Lord prohibited them from marrying wives who would turn their hearts away from Him (Deuteronomy 17:17). God had nothing against foreigners *per se*, but often a foreign spouse brought along a belief in a foreign god.

King Solomon literally wrote the book on wisdom. And yet, he behaved so foolishly in the realm of matrimony! How? It started with a small compromise: "Solomon formed a marriage alliance with Pharaoh king of Egypt" (1 Kings 3:1). Solomon's marriage to an unbeliever was an attempt to buy national security for the price of a wedding. This small sin opened a crack in Solomon's heart that eventually divided it. Eight chapters later we read what seems inconceivable: Solomon had "seven hundred wives, princesses, and three hundred concubines, and his wives turned his heart away" (1 Kings 11:3). He let his wives worship their gods in the land of the true God, and it wasn't long before Solomon joined in (11:1–8).

That tally wasn't a typo. How could Solomon remember a thousand women? (Maybe with nametags: "Hello, my name is . . .") The king should have seen disaster coming. Even his own poetry warned of guarding one's heart and dealing with sin while it's small (Proverbs 4:23; 17:14; 24:33–34; Ecclesiastes 10:18; Song of Solomon 2:15). Solomon never started out to worship pagan gods. But the crack that divided his heart would ultimately divide his nation, destroy God's temple, and deport the Hebrews into exile (Nehemiah 13:26). And it all began with a marriage to a foreign woman . . . that led to more unbelieving wives . . . and then to more.

God's standards haven't changed. The New Testament reiterates that a Christian should only marry another believer—one who can bear the weight of a life of faith (2 Corinthians 6:14). God knows that a spouse can influence the heart of his or her partner—either for good or for evil.

—Wayne Stiles

The Rest of the Story: Read 1 Kings 11:1–13.

Take It to *Heart*

Is there a specific area of choices—perhaps dating, engagement, marriage, or elsewhere—where you should guard your heart, even when the decisions seem small? What choices are you facing today that have potentially far-reaching impact?

_____

_____

_____

_____

_____

_____

_____

_____

_____

_____

_____

_____

_____

_____

_____

There was no one like Ahab who sold himself to do evil in the sight of the LORD, because Jezebel his wife incited him.

— 1 Kings 21:25

Jezebel
LOSING CONTROL BY SEIZING IT

Nobody names their little girl Jezebel anymore, and no woman would ever want to be called a Jezebel. The life of this powerful woman is a warning of what could go wrong when we insist, "I *will* have my way."

Jezebel and her husband Ahab lived in a spiritually dry time in Israel's history. When the nation was divided, Ahab ruled the northern kingdom. When he chose Jezebel, a foreign, pagan woman, as his wife, he turned a blind eye to her revival of Baal worship in Israel. No surprise then that she eventually turned Ahab's heart away from God (1 Kings 16:28–33).

No doubt Jezebel was a strong and savvy woman. Regardless of Ahab's role as king, she wore the pants in the family. Adopting a *whatever-it-takes* mentality to get her way, she made evil men quake and good men run (19:2–3).

Nothing was too big or too sacred to stand in her way:

When her husband wanted to expand their garden, she plotted against their neighbor, had him stoned to death, and took his land (21:5–7, 15).

When godly priests refused to bow their knee to her idol Baal, she had them wiped out (18:4).

When the prophet Elijah called her what she was, he took first place on her Most Wanted list (1 Kings 19:1–2).

Even her husband the king, strong in battle, couldn't live up to her expectation and feared her disdain.

For Jezebel, high ambition became a madness, and in her pride, she believed she was unstoppable. But, as in all of history, there came a day when God said, *Enough*.

In patient grace, the Lord puts evil men and women on a leash, giving them enough length to turn on their own from their evil ways. When they don't, God steps in. And His word is final. Nothing can frustrate God's plan.

Jezebel's life ended quite unceremoniously when she was pushed out a window. No one picked up her body, and eventually dogs devoured her, just like God said they would (2 Kings 9:30–37).

If your confidence has turned into the need to control, the lesson from Jezebel's life is hard to swallow: don't be fooled into thinking *your* plan is under *your* control. The world may call that power and influence, but God calls it wickedness. And it will take you to a very bad place in a heartbeat.

Today is the day to humble yourself under His hand. Don't wait for God to force you to your knees.

—Barb Peil

The Rest of the Story: Read 1 Kings 16–21.

Take It to *Heart*

Ask yourself: do I manipulate people or circumstances—even subtly—to get my way? What situations am I trying to control right now? Do I rationalize away even the slightest tinge of conviction? "Search me, O God . . . see if there be any wicked way in me" (Psalm 139:23–24 KJV).

When she came to the man of God to the hill, she caught hold of [Elisha's] feet. And Gehazi came near to push her away; but the man of God said, "Let her alone, for her soul is troubled within her; and the Lord has hidden it from me and has not told me."

— 2 Kings 4:27

The Shunammite Woman

PERSEVERING IN GOOD TIMES AND BAD

In the village of Shunem, there lived a woman who saw the great prophet Elisha passing by one day and insisted he take rest and eat at her home. Eventually, the Shunammite and her husband built Elisha a small room onto their home where he could rest from his journeys. Grateful for her ministry, Elisha prayed that God would bless the barren woman with a son.

Many years later, when the boy was old enough to work in the fields at the harvest, he suffered an injury, possibly sunstroke, and died shortly afterward. The Shunammite ran off immediately to find the prophet. First, she met Elisha's servant and told him all was well—a remarkable show of trust in God and His prophet Elisha to deal mercifully with her. Upon meeting Elisha himself, she threw herself at his feet, and rather than complain or berate him, merely asked whether she had requested a son from him all those years before. Knowing then that something had gone terribly wrong, Elisha went and raised the boy from the dead.

The Shunammite's faith was the means God used to bring great blessing to her family, first in giving her a son, then in raising that son from the dead. The Shunammite understood the importance of persevering in her faith, no matter the circumstances of life. Her faith taught her to look not only to her own needs but also to the needs of others. And when the circumstances of life turned against her, rather than turn inward to rely on herself, she continued her practice of looking outward and upward, relying on her Lord and His prophet Elisha. She persevered in her faith through the good times and the bad.

This is the kind of trust we all need and desire, isn't it? The kind of conviction that is so practiced it perseveres whether or not life goes our way. It's a faith that bursts forth with fresh vibrancy as we care for the needs of others. It deals with the trials of life that are sure to come. This faith we all desire and should be striving for is the same devotion the apostle James called us to, a mature faith that evidences itself in our actions, no matter the circumstances of our lives (James 2:23).

—John Adair

The Rest of the Story: Read 2 Kings 4:8–37; 8:1–6.

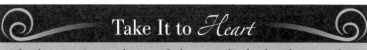

Take It to *Heart*

Whether you're in the good days or the bad right now, how can you better cling to your faith as the Shunammite woman did? What choices must you make in your relationship with the Lord and in your relationships with others to better exhibit a life of faith?

_____

_____

_____

_____

_____

_____

_____

_____

_____

_____

_____

_____

_____

_____

_____

_____

"For if you remain silent at this time, relief and deliverance will arise for the Jews from another place and you and your father's house will perish. And who knows whether you have not attained royalty for such a time as this?"

—Esther 4:14

Esther
WAITING ON GOD TO WORK

A silent yet powerful interlude occurs between chapters four and five of the ancient book of Esther. In that epochal moment, the ancient world held its breath.

Esther, the lovely Jewish woman whom God had placed in the king's palace, had just sent word to her Uncle Mordecai. In three days, she planned to enter the king's presence uninvited and plead for the lives of God's people. She literally would break the law by interrupting the king. This could have meant her instant death. That is chapter four.

Then came a grand pause . . . time hung in the balance. In this white space between her bold decision in chapter four and her dangerous action three days later in chapter five, Esther drew on the source of her strength. Suspend for a moment the outcome that you know will come. Nothing is recorded about this time except Esther's request for Mordecai to "assemble all the Jews who are found in Susa, and fast for me . . . for three days, night or day. I and my maidens also will fast in the same way. And thus I will go in to the king, which is not according to the law; and if I perish, I perish" (Esther 4:16).

During this time of fasting, Esther undoubtedly waited on her Lord in prayer. She filled the time normally spent on meals with protracted periods of prayer and silent fasting. In other words, she determined to wait on the Lord and allowed Him to guide her thoughts and help frame her words for that moment when her life was at risk—and subsequently the lives of thousands of God's people.

Now, in the quiet space between these two chapters, don't think for a moment that God was absent. Remember, He may be invisible in this story, but He was at work. He can be moving in a thousand places at once without ever being noticed.

As the Lord gripped Esther's heart, she became unafraid of what she faced. It was a silent yet powerful parenthesis in her life. God honored it.

—Charles R. Swindoll

The Rest of the Story: Read the book of Esther.

Take It to *Heart*

Perhaps you are in one of those "white spaces" right now. If so, it's time for you to pray and fast and call upon a few close friends to join you. If you don't know your way through an unpredictable situation, if you can't find the path to walk, if the Lord seems invisible in your story, *wait* . . . and give this time to God. He is the One who provides strength for the next step. How? He whispers reassurance to us through His Word and deepens our determination through His Spirit to do what is right. When we wait on the Lord, those "white spaces" become the light that guides our steps. Write a prayer here.

_____

_____

_____

_____

_____

_____

_____

_____

_____

_____

_____

Charm is deceitful and beauty is vain,
But a woman who fears the LORD, she shall
be praised.

—Proverbs 31:30

The Virtuous Woman

PLEASING THE LORD MOST OF ALL

Relax.

Proverbs 31 is not God's performance manual for today's Christian woman — though at times it feels downright intimidating. Nor is it a handbook about how to get more done in your day. Who could measure up to this virtuous superwoman? No, God knows what women need in order to walk with Him, and it's not motivation by comparison or godliness by exhaustion.

This well-known and often quoted section of Proverbs is dedicated to the countless women who live busy, fruitful lives without a crowd's applause and often even without anyone's notice. The writer, an unknown man named Lemuel, wanted us to know, without a doubt, that God sees our lives. Juggling all her responsibilities, it's the faithfulness of a woman's life that matters to God.

And so in this book dedicated to living wisely, we get a pencil sketch of a woman's daily life that pleases the Lord. In its original language, this section of Proverbs 31 is laid out as an acrostic to assist in memorization. And by looking at the life of this biblical woman, today's woman on the go can learn three secrets for success:

Secret #1: A virtuous woman lives intentionally.

A woman who pleases the Lord goes after life. She works hard, in and out of the home. She works smart, making good deals and wise investments with both her time and money. She doesn't spin her wheels with worry or fear. She doesn't look back.

Secret #2: A virtuous woman cares for others.

What's in it for me? doesn't cross her mind. Instead, it's *What's best for you?* Strong and capable, a woman who pleases the Lord is easy for her husband to lead. Unselfish and generous, her hands are open, sharing food or values or counsel — whatever is the need of the moment. Her heart is open and her spirit is kind — loving in quiet, thoughtful, sacrificial ways. She's not consumed with herself.

Secret #3: A virtuous woman knows that the most important thing about her is how she relates to God.

Looks and personality make great first impressions but their influence fades with time. Accomplishments may also impress for a while, but the thing that pleases the Lord about a woman is not visible on the outside. It's her relationship with Him that matters; the same is true for you. At the end of the day when your head hits the pillow and you release that tired, contented sigh, being a Proverbs 31 woman means pleading with God every day to help you please Him most of all.

— *Barb Peil*

The Rest of the Story: Read Proverbs 31:10–31.

Take It to *Heart*

Decide what kind of woman you're going to be and then be that. That may mean shifting around some priorities in your life. Look at your schedule. Look at your budget. Look at your home and relationships. Ask the Lord to reveal the areas that need to change in order for you to please Him most of all.

While they were [in Bethlehem], the days were completed for her to give birth. And she gave birth to her firstborn son; and she wrapped Him in cloths, and laid Him in a manger, because there was no room for them in the inn.

—Luke 2:6–7

Mary, Mother of Jesus

SURRENDERING TO GOD'S PURPOSES

When Mary and Joseph first began their journey southward to Bethlehem, they may have felt sure they had time to make the trip, register for the census, and then return home to Nazareth. The weather cooperated and a donkey carried their provisions, but the journey proved more difficult than either of them had expected. Mary was soon to give birth.

By the time they reached Bethlehem, Mary was exhausted. To make matters worse, the tiny town was burgeoning with people. Joseph searched for lodging, but none could be found. One kind family agreed to put them up in a stable. It was a crude shelter, but it kept them out of the elements and a low fire warmed the chilly night air.

I imagine that once they were settled, Mary rested while Joseph worked his way through the corrupt registration process. Too soon, a powerful, dull ache gripped Mary's waist. She called for Joseph in a panic, but he would be gone for hours. She had attended many childbirths, so she calmed herself and arranged their little shelter in preparation for the baby. A spare tunic would be His swaddling; a little bed in the feeding trough with fresh straw would cradle Him.

As evening fell, her labor intensified. I picture Joseph returning to find Mary moaning through a wave of pain. There are no pains like those of childbirth. None so intense. None so hopeful. Only the reminder that she would soon be holding her baby kept her focused.

It was well into the night when Joseph laid the tiny Hope of Israel across Mary's tummy. For nine months, Mary had talked to Him, sung to Him, felt His body move, and looked forward to the day when she could finally touch Him. Now she held Him in her arms—Immanuel . . . "God with us" (Matthew 1:23). Perhaps in that moment she remembered the angel who had visited her nine months earlier, saying, "Do not be afraid, Mary" (Luke 1:30).

I wonder if in those first hours, God gave Mary a brief premonition of years to come, when another would point to her Son and say, "Behold, the Lamb of God who takes away the sin of the world" (John 1:29) . . . and then of the day that would come when a sword of emotion would pierce her own soul (Luke 2:35). Yes, those days would surely come. The little Lamb that was born was destined for sacrifice. But tonight Mary just held her baby close and cried softly in the wonder of it all.

—*Charles R. Swindoll*

The Rest of the Story: Read Luke 2.

From the day she learned of God's plan, Mary's attitude had been one of submission to God. What situation do you face today that can be offered to God with open hands? *Whatever You want, Lord . . .*

_____

_____

_____

_____

_____

_____

_____

_____

_____

_____

_____

_____

_____

_____

_____

_____

_____

_____

[Zacharias and Elizabeth] were both righteous in the sight of God, walking blamelessly in all the commandments and requirements of the Lord. But they had no child, because Elizabeth was barren, and they were both advanced in years.

—Luke 1:6–7

Elizabeth
REJOICING IN GOD'S BLESSING

It was a momentous year for Elizabeth. When her husband, Zacharias, went up to Jerusalem for his priestly service, he received the once-in-a-lifetime honor of entering the temple to burn incense and pray for his people. But even the privilege of serving in the temple paled in comparison to what Zacharias found inside: the angel Gabriel announcing that Zacharias and Elizabeth would soon be parents.

By this time, Elizabeth was old enough to believe that she and Zacharias would never have children. This would have been a great disappointment, and no doubt her barrenness weighed on her. But despite that, she and Zacharias remained righteous and blameless before the Lord. Even this misfortune had not deterred her from walking with God as the years passed (Luke 1:6). Indeed, immediately after becoming pregnant, Elizabeth gave God the credit for the blessing of new life in what had been a dead womb: "This is the way the Lord has dealt with me in the days when He looked with favor upon me, to take away my disgrace among men" (1:25).

Still three months away from giving birth to her baby boy, Elizabeth received yet another honor. Upon welcoming her young cousin Mary into her home, "Elizabeth was filled with the Holy Spirit" and had the privilege of pronouncing a blessing on Mary and the unborn baby Jesus still growing in her womb: "Blessed are you among women, and blessed is the fruit of your womb!" (Luke 1:42).

As the barren wife of a priest, Elizabeth could have chosen to sink into bitterness during her empty childbearing years. Instead, she remained faithful. Her response to Mary's visit and to her own pregnancy made it clear that her life was defined by joy, rather than a lingering resentment that might have caused her to cry, "It's about time!"

When disappointments come, it can be difficult to remain close to the Lord. The temptation for us is to turn away from Him in those times, to acquire a hardened mind-set that will protect us from the pain of our circumstances. The account of Elizabeth provides a strong counter to that temptation. She waited through those barren years and walked blamelessly with God, regardless of God's manifest blessing on her life.

—John Adair

The Rest of the Story: Read Luke 1:5–45.

How has bitterness over a painful experience in your past prevented you from truly enjoying God's blessing in your life? Take a moment to thank Him for what He has blessed you with, regardless of what He has not.

_____

_____

_____

_____

_____

_____

_____

_____

_____

_____

_____

_____

_____

_____

_____

_____

_____

_____

[Anna] never left the temple, serving night and day with fastings and prayers.

— Luke 2:37

Anna
Praying until It Happens

One of the great mysteries of God is how prayer changes the world.

Luke 2 tells us that prayer was a secret that Anna kept. A prophetess "advanced in years," she worshiped in the temple, fasting and praying night and day. Like shadows cast from the Old Testament into the early pages of the New Testament, Anna, along with the old man Simeon, was among the faithful who patiently, passionately, and expectantly prayed for the One to come who would redeem Israel. One day had knitted into another until the years gathered like knots on a prayer shawl. Anna and Simeon wrapped themselves in God's promise and kept pleading in His throne room year after year.

And then the day arrived. Anna showed up in the temple that morning as she had for as many as eight decades. Picture her, a fixture on the temple mount for as long as anyone remembered. The morning light, reflecting off the high walls, cast her in a golden spotlight as she took her familiar post along the archways. Her day's work of prayer lay ahead. Then she noticed them. Over there. The young couple talking to Simeon. The child in his arms. The tears running down his face. She knew in a moment. Her wrinkled hand flew over her mouth and then both hands flew over her head, *Praise be to God! He's here! The Messiah has come!*

On the day that Mary and Joseph walked into the temple to present their newborn Jesus to the Lord, Anna and Simeon's long-prayed petition was answered: the "salvation / Which You have prepared in the presence of all peoples, / A light of revelation to the Gentiles, / And the glory of Your people Israel" (Luke 2:30–32). Mary and Joseph marveled at what the two faithful ones said about the baby. Anna could only give "thanks to God, and . . . speak of [Jesus] to all those who were looking for the redemption of Jerusalem" (2:38). Likely, no one could get the old gal to hush . . . *and rightly so!*

A lifetime's request was answered; the Messiah had finally come. Exactly how Anna's prayers factored into God's perfect timing can be trusted to His sovereignty. It is enough to note that Anna had been faithful to pray—to believe God would be true to His Word, even when days stretched to months . . . then to years . . . and even to decades. Anna learned a secret about prayer, one all of God's people who wait on Him know. Yes, God changes the world through prayer . . . don't give up.

—Barb Peil

The Rest of the Story: Read Luke 2.

Take It to *Heart*

Have you been praying for something for decades? Stay at it. Keep believing that God is at work. Even now, commit that need or desire to the Lord once again with fresh faith stirred by these two faithful people of prayer.

Herodias had a grudge against [John] and wanted to put him to death.

—Mark 6:19

Herodias

HARBORING VINDICTIVE CRUELTY

Tracing Herodias's genealogy is like tracking the gnarled and tangled roots of a poisonous tree. Her life and family were marked by cunningness, deceit, immorality, and murder. Her family had planted the seed of wickedness; now it bore wicked fruit.

Herodias's grandfather, Herod the Great—the destroyer of innocent children in Bethlehem after the birth of Jesus—gave her in marriage to Herod's son, Philip, her half-uncle. Later she divorced Philip and entered into another incestuous and illicit union with Philip's half-brother, Herod Antipas, the governor of Galilee and Peraea. John the Baptist condemned Antipas for marrying his half-sister, saying, "It is not lawful for you to have your brother's wife" (Mark 6:18). John's denunciation enraged them, and both Antipas and Herodias wanted John dead. Antipas, however, "knowing that [John] was a righteous and holy man" (6:20) and fearing John's power over the large crowds, only had him arrested.

Vindictive and cruel, Herodias meant to have John's head, so she laid a trap for Antipas, using her own teenage daughter as bait. Herodias sprung the trap when her "victim" least expected it—when Antipas was merry at the celebration of his birthday. Thrust onto the stage to dance in front of the lords and military men who had come to join in the birthday revelry,

Herodias's daughter thrilled the men, especially the governor who told her he would give her any birthday gift she wanted. All she need do was ask.

Not knowing what to ask for, the young woman asked her mother. Here the viper struck: ask for "the head of John the Baptist" (Mark 6:24). Antipas was "sorry" but granted the request and immediately delivered John's head on a platter.

Herodias was a woman seething with bitter anger—an unsavory poisonous fruit of revenge. Once infected with the venom of vengeance, the only antivenom for the soul is forgiveness.

Herodias's life teaches us the truth that a family tree planted in wickedness will produce a harvest of sin, unless an axe is taken to the poisonous root. The sin we excuse in moderation, rest assured, our children will excuse in excess. To halt this production of sin, we need to graft into our lives a branch of divine forgiveness, which only comes through faith in Christ and obedience to Him.

—*Derrick G. Jeter*

The Rest of the Story: Read Matthew 2:13, 16 and Mark 6:17–28.

Has someone ever put a mirror in front of you so that you could see sin in your life? How did you respond? How should you have responded? Have you ever been wronged and wished you could've extracted vengeance? Write about these questions and your answers in light of Romans 12:17–20.

Martha then said to Jesus, "Lord, if You had been here, my brother would not have died."

—John 11:21

Mary and Martha

Mary and Martha sent a message to Jesus that their brother Lazarus lay sick. The journey to Bethany would've taken Jesus two days of hard, hot, uphill walking. But instead of immediately traveling to Bethany, Jesus stayed right where He was beyond the Jordan River. When He finally did arrive, Lazarus had been dead four days. In other words, Jesus had taken His sweet time showing up.

"Lord, if You had been here," Martha cried, "my brother would not have died" (John 11:21). When Mary later approached Jesus, she fell at His feet and echoed Martha's grief, word for word, through bitter tears: "Lord, if You had been here, my brother would not have died" (11:32). The sisters' words revealed their faith in Jesus's ability . . . but also their disappointment in His delay. Their assumption? Because Jesus *could have* saved Lazarus, He *should have*.

Pain often tempts us to view Jesus this way. But this story reveals that the exact opposite is true. It wasn't Jesus's lack of concern that caused His delay; rather, it was His *love* for the sisters and for Lazarus (John 11:5–6).

As hard as we try, wrapping our minds around that seeming contradiction is still a struggle. After all, it's hard to feel God's love when we've cried out to Him, perhaps for years, and

He seems to ignore us. Our pain blurs what Jesus sees clearly. That's what happened with Mary and Martha. Jesus saw what they couldn't through the haze of their hurt. He knew what Lazarus's death would produce—an opportunity for nonbelievers to witness a miracle. Jesus knew that Mary and Martha would grow to understand that God loved them on a level that went deeper than simply removing their pain and answering their shortsighted request.

Those lessons apply to you as well. Because Jesus waited, you can know He wants to give you more than relief. Because Jesus wept, you can know He feels your pain, strengthening you with His presence along the path that He in His sovereign will sees as best for you. He loves you enough to delay the answer and even to let you hurt—so that you will gain what you could not otherwise. Jesus walks with you—and weeps—along the painful road that leads to death . . . but also to resurrection.

—Wayne Stiles

The Rest of the Story: Read John 11:1–44.

In what circumstance today do you find yourself continuing to wait on God? Can you praise Him in spite of your disappointment? Does it help to know that His delay represents His love, not His indifference?

_____

_____

_____

_____

_____

_____

_____

_____

_____

_____

_____

_____

_____

_____

_____

_____

_____

A Canaanite woman from that region came out and began to cry out, saying, "Have mercy on me, Lord, Son of David; my daughter is cruelly demon-possessed." But He did not answer her a word. And His disciples came and implored Him, saying, "Send her away, because she keeps shouting at us."

—Matthew 15:22–23

The Syrophoenician Woman

PLEADING FOR GRACE

To the Jews she was no better than a dog—a mangy, disease-infected, scavenger—who deserved only a kick from the sole of a sandal or a whack from the end of a stick. She certainly didn't merit the time and attention of a rabbi like Jesus. Yet, He gave her so much more.

After teaching in the territory of the Galilee, Jesus took His disciples into a region that they would have considered unclean, a place unfit for a proper Jew—the Gentile region of Tyre and Sidon. While there, a Canaanite—or Syrophoenician—woman came to Jesus, begging Him to heal her demon-possessed daughter (Mark 7:25–26). No doubt she had heard of Jesus's miraculous ministry of healing, and now finding herself desperate, she took the opportunity to seek a small miracle from the Jewish miracle worker.

The scene was quite dramatic. She relentlessly cried out: "Have mercy on me, [O] Lord, Son of David; my daughter is cruelly demon-possessed" (Matthew 15:22). And on and on the woman cried. But Jesus would not answer her pleas for help, and the disciples became annoyed with her. They pressed Jesus to "send her away" because she was persistently pestering them with her shouting (Matthew 15:23). It was then that Jesus turned to the woman and informed her that He had come as Israel's Messiah and that blessings should be fed first to the children of the Jews before the "dogs" of the Gentiles were fed (Matthew 15:24, 26).

She wasn't offended by the term *dogs*. She knew she was outside the Jewish family. But coming to Jesus in humble and desperate dependence, trusting in His grace alone, she answered with wisdom and faith—"even the dogs feed on the crumbs which fall from their masters' table" (15:27). She was only asking for a small blessing—the healing of her innocent daughter. Couldn't the Master at least drop that crumb from the table? Jesus's response was a feast of grace: "O woman, your faith is great; it shall be done for you as you wish" (15:28). And so it was.

The grace of Christ is for everyone, freely given to those who come to Him in faith. The urgency of this woman's need— the healing of her child—is a model of how we, too, should depend on Christ's grace. We may boldly come, yet with humility, recognizing that our need is greater than our ability . . . but not too great for His.

—Derrick G. Jeter

The Rest of the Story: Read Matthew 15:21–28.

Take It to *Heart*

Have you ever come to Christ in faith, seeking His grace for a desperate need? Explain. Whom do you know who might be like the Syrophoenician woman—someone others consider an outsider? How can you be an agent of grace in this person's life?

_____

_____

_____

_____

_____

_____

_____

_____

_____

_____

_____

_____

_____

From that city many of the Samaritans believed in Him because of the word of the woman who testified, "He told me all the things that I have done."

—John 4:39

The Samaritan Woman

LOOKING FOR LOVE IN ALL THE WRONG PLACES

Soft footsteps approached the well where Jesus sat alone. He turned to see a water jar on the head of a solitary woman—a Samaritan. Jesus smiled; she stared awkwardly. Then Jesus did the unthinkable: He spoke to her.

"Give Me a drink" (John 4:7).

With those words, Jesus crossed major cultural barriers. As the apostle John reminded us: "Jews have no dealings with Samaritans" (4:9). She asked why He, a Jewish man, would speak to her, a Samaritan woman. Any other Jew would have gone thirsty. But Jesus wasn't any other Jew.

"If you knew the gift of God," Jesus replied, "and who it is who says to you, 'Give Me a drink,' you would have asked Him, and He would have given you living water" (4:10). In other words, the cultural barrier couldn't compare to the spiritual barrier Jesus crossed. God had come to a sinner.

Jesus explained that "living water" refers to spiritual life, and then He revealed her need for it: "Go, call your husband and come here."

"I have no husband," she shot back.

"You have had five husbands," Jesus declared, "and the one whom you now have is not your husband" (John 4:16–18).

His words felt like an emotional slap. Talk about revealing a need! She had tried to hide her sin . . . but God still found her. He always does.

Then and now, the world makes promises it can't keep. It claims that the reason we're unhappy is because we just haven't found the right spouse, the right haircut or conditioner, the right salary or neighborhood, the right expression of our creativity, the right church, the right Bible study, *ad infinitum . . . ad nauseam*.

Even those who believe in Jesus can toss their buckets down the wrong wells. But God doesn't let us run from reality; He loves us too much. He'll prod us—even pierce us—to lead us to the truth that God alone remains the source of fulfillment and motivation in the deepest part of our hearts. He alone satisfies.

The Samaritan woman had sought purpose and security in relationships. Jesus's words to her—"Everyone who drinks of this water will thirst again" (4:13)—apply to more than merely water. They relate to everything—*everything*—we draw from in life for meaning and fulfillment apart from the One who spoke the words.

—*Wayne Stiles*

The Rest of the Story: Read John 4:1–42.

Can any person or position or possession ever satisfy? What well are you drawing from today that only makes you thirst again?

_____

_____

_____

_____

_____

_____

_____

_____

_____

_____

_____

_____

_____

_____

_____

_____

_____

Now on the first day of the week Mary Magdalene came early to the tomb, while it was still dark, and saw the stone already taken away from the tomb.

—John 20:1

Mary Magdalene

When Mary showed up at Jesus's grave early that Sunday morning and saw the empty tomb, she was probably already overdone. A weekend of grief had followed the horrible day when she had watched the most important person in her life suffer an excruciating death. It's no wonder that at the first sight of what she assumed was vandalism of His grave, she just melted down.

The scene makes us smile sympathetically, reminding us why we should adore Mary Magdalene. Simply, because she was there. It was early and dark—a setting full of sorrow—yet Mary showed up to serve just like she had at every significant event in Jesus's public ministry.

Mary Magdalene had followed Jesus from way back when. Her name tells us she was from Magdela, a town around the lake Jesus called home. It was most likely there that Jesus had rescued her from the seven demons that had terrorized her soul. When He gave her back her life, she returned it to Him and followed Him from that day forward.

Luke 8 tells us that Mary and several other women followed Jesus—even privately funding the Teacher and His men as they proclaimed and preached "the kingdom of God from one city to another" (Luke 8:1). In between listening to Jesus teach, the women cooked; they ministered and served; they did what they could to keep Jesus's mission moving forward.

What didn't make it into the Gospels was all the camaraderie that the group no doubt enjoyed in Jesus's company. Bound together in heart and mission, the men's laughter and crazy stories over firelight probably echoed across the water in Galilee and made Mary and the other women smile and roll their eyes. This group knew Jesus like no one else did, and they loved Him all the more.

That's why Mary showed up at the tomb with burial spices that Easter morning—to serve her Friend and Teacher one last time in solemn, loving duty. She followed to the end.

But it wasn't the end.

The Lord was especially kind to Mary that early morning when He chose to appear to her *first*, even before the disciples, and to call her by name . . . *Mary*. Can you imagine what she felt as she looked into that stranger's face . . . and saw her Lord?

—*Barb Peil*

The Rest of the Story: Read John 20.

Take a quiet look around at your company of friends. Do you find a Mary? Are you a Mary—quietly, lovingly serving the Lord? Our lesson from Mary's life is perseverance. Keep at it, Mary. The Lord sees your hard work. He who set you free, calls you still to follow.

Calling His disciples to Him, He said to them, "Truly I say to you, this poor widow put in more than all the contributors to the treasury; for they all put in out of their surplus, but she, out of her poverty, put in all she owned, all she had to live on."

—Mark 12:43–44

The Widow with Mites
GIVING EVERYTHING SHE HAD

A widow in first-century Jerusalem had few options when it came to providing for her daily needs. Even if she had a father or other family still living with whom she could take refuge, as an unmarried woman, she wouldn't have just been able to go out and get a full-time job to support herself. Therefore, actual money would have rarely come to a widow outside of another's charity.

So the walk up and down streets on the way to the temple treasury would have likely been a rare trip for this widow — she just didn't have money that often. But one day, somehow, the widow had received two mites (copper coins). And instead of spending the money on something for herself — a new headscarf or groceries or some needed home item — her faith impelled her to give both coins to the Lord.

She likely stood out among the much richer people giving to the treasury that day. While she had, no doubt, made an effort to keep her dress looking fresh, the shabbiness of her clothes would have been unmistakable. But with her head held high in noble dignity, she dropped her two tiny coins — worth about half-a-cent each — into the treasury. With all the jangling of coins from those giving out of their surplus, hers would have gone without notice to those around her — as if she'd put nothing in the box.

However, Jesus was watching. He proclaimed that she did more than just put *something* into the box: the "poor widow put in more than all the contributors to the treasury," for "she, out of her poverty, put in all she owned, all she had to live on" (Mark 12:43–44). Her unshakable trust in the Lord enabled her to give everything she had for His glory.

In a world where "image is everything," a widow who gave her last two mites stands as a striking example of the substance that true faith brings to our lives. This is not a faith built on spiritual platitudes but one that seeks to actually *live* as Christ did during His time on earth — giving to others, even at great sacrifice to ourselves. If we hope to live out our faith as He did, we, too, must surrender to His control everything we have — financially and otherwise — and trust in Him to take care of our every need.

— John Adair

The Rest of the Story: Read Mark 12:41–44.

What parts of your life have you resisted giving over completely to the Lord? Take a few moments and surrender everything to Him.

_____

_____

_____

_____

_____

_____

_____

_____

_____

_____

_____

_____

_____

_____

_____

_____

The Lord opened [Lydia's] heart to respond to the things spoken by Paul. And when she and her household had been baptized, she urged us, saying, "If you have judged me to be faithful to the Lord, come into my house and stay." And she prevailed upon us.

—Acts 16:14–15

Lydia

OPENING HER HEART AND HER HOME TO GOD

Lydia made her way outside the city gate. A short stroll led her and a group of women to a familiar spot beside the Gangites River. For a synagogue to be established, ten Jewish men had to be in regular attendance. There weren't ten to be found in Philippi. That didn't keep these women from worshiping together, though. They gathered every Saturday at the river for prayer.

But this Sabbath was different . . . it would change Lydia's life forever.

A company of strangers approached the river. After exchanging pleasantries with the ladies, the men sat down and began talking about Jesus of Nazareth, the one who had come as the promised Messiah. As Lydia listened to the man named Paul speak, his words stirred her heart like none she had heard before. So many of the prophecies she knew from the Scriptures suddenly made sense. She responded to Paul's words—as did her whole household. In that moment, they believed in Jesus.

The Lord not only opened Lydia's heart to respond to Paul's message, but He also opened her heart to respond to the needs of the travelers. Her simple invitation revealed her generosity: "If you have judged me to be faithful to the Lord, come into my house and stay" (Acts 16:15). As a merchant of fine purple cloth, Lydia could afford generous hospitality, and her home could easily accommodate Paul and his companions. At Lydia's insistence, they lodged in her house. Moreover, her home eventually became a place where local Christians gathered together (Acts 16:40).

Lydia's hospitality may have even served as the catalyst for the generous, giving spirit of the new church Paul established in Philippi. Years later, when the apostle wrote to the Philippian church, he recalled their generosity at his initial meeting with them:

> You yourselves also know, Philippians, that at the first preaching of the gospel, after I left Macedonia, no church shared with me in the matter of giving and receiving but you alone. (Philippians 4:15)

No doubt Lydia was part of those early gifts. She understood that when God redeemed her life, every part of who she was became His—her heart, her home, her time, and her treasure.

Lydia serves as a marvelous model of one who recognized that our worship of God can be expressed with *anything* we choose to offer Him. For, as Paul expressed regarding the Philippians' generous financial gift to him, it was "a fragrant aroma, an acceptable sacrifice, well-pleasing to God" (4:18).

— *Wayne Stiles*

The Rest of the Story: Read Acts 16:11–15.

Take It to *Heart*

What do you have to offer the Lord in worship today—your heart, your home, your time, your treasure?

_____

_____

_____

_____

_____

_____

_____

_____

_____

_____

_____

_____

_____

_____

_____

_____

_____

_____

_____

_____

When Priscilla and Aquila heard [Apollos], they took him aside and explained to him the way of God more accurately.

—Acts 18:26

Priscilla
ADDING ACCURACY TO ELOQUENCE

Other than the apostles, Priscilla stands as one of the great teachers of the Christian faith during the New Testament era. What made her great? She longed for truth to be taught accurately.

She first came on the biblical scene with her husband Aquila. They were Jewish Christians on the run from their former home in Rome, leaving the great city after the emperor Claudius issued his famous edict expelling all Jews from the city. Priscilla and her husband met Paul in Corinth and, because they were all tentmakers by trade, they invited the apostle to stay with them.

Eventually, Priscilla, Aquila, and Paul all made for Ephesus, where Paul left the couple to minister to the Christians in the city. Sometime after the apostle left Ephesus, a Jewish Christian named Apollos came to the city and began preaching about Christ. Apollos was quite the notable preacher. Luke described him as "eloquent," "mighty in the Scriptures," and "fervent in spirit" (Acts 18:24–25). However, when Priscilla and Aquila heard Apollos, they immediately understood that he needed further teaching, so they "explained to him the way of God more accurately" (18:26).

Priscilla believed that right doctrine and sound teaching mattered. This should come as no surprise, as her mentor Paul emphasized the same principle to one of his other protégés, young Timothy (2 Timothy 2:15). Priscilla believed in sound doctrine so fervently that, even in the presence of the eloquent Apollos, she and her husband had the courage and care to approach him so that they might expand his knowledge and understanding of the Christian faith.

Too often we give doctrine the short shrift, preferring good feelings, peppy music, and an engaging preacher to truth that is taught accurately. But the fact remains that our faith is meaningless if we don't know the one, true God our Father and Jesus Christ His Son, who died on the cross and was raised from the dead for the sake of human beings everywhere. If we, like Priscilla, make the commitment to loving God with our minds as well as we do with our hearts, we, too, might enjoy an effective and long-standing impact among God's people.

—John Adair

The Rest of the Story: Read Acts 18:1–4, 18–28.

Take It to *Heart*

How does your faith increase when you're presented with doctrine, such as truth about God and His Word and the world? How does Priscilla's commitment to teaching the truth change your perception of doctrine?

_____

_____

_____

_____

_____

_____

_____

_____

_____

_____

_____

_____

_____

_____

_____

You, however, continue in the things you have learned and become convinced of, knowing from whom you have learned them, and that from childhood you have known the sacred writings which are able to give you the wisdom that leads to salvation through faith which is in Christ Jesus.

—2 Timothy 3:14–15

Eunice and Lois

PASSING ON GRACE TO A NEW GENERATION

It's easy to think of the people we meet in the Bible as having been reared by the best of parents in the most ideal of homes. Hardly. I'm sure if Timothy had been interviewed by some reporter, he would have sighed when asked about his childhood. Timothy's home had been a divided one; his Jewish mother and Greek father did not see eye-to-eye on spiritual matters. Timothy's father came from a pagan background, and his mother, Eunice, had been influenced by her godly mother, Lois.

As often is the case with the influence of mothers (and grandmothers!), these two women had a tremendous impact on young Timothy's life. Through the pen of Paul the apostle, we see snapshots of the lingering legacy of these influential women.

Paul wrote to Timothy, "I [am] . . . longing to see you, even as I recall your tears, so that I may be filled with joy" (2 Timothy 1:4). Children do not usually learn tenderness from their father; they usually get it from their mothers. Timothy was no exception. His tears were not from embarrassment or regret. They were healthy tears from a secure life. He was openly vulnerable, with a tenderness that was essential for his role as pastor. Thanks to these "real" women, Timothy was authentically caring of his people. Eunice and Lois deposited genuine tenderness into their young man's life. Mothers help soften our spirits. They model compassion and tenderness better than fathers ever could.

Timothy received the valuable inheritance of faith from Eunice and Lois. He must have been encouraged as he read Paul's letter to him: "Continue in the things you have learned and become convinced of, knowing from whom you have learned them, and that from childhood you have known the sacred writings which are able to give you the wisdom that leads to salvation through faith which is in Christ Jesus" (2 Timothy 3:14–15). Once again, Paul reminded the young man, *You got this faith from your mother! You became convinced of your firm convictions from her example.* Our mothers are the first to determine our convictions: "Children, this is where we're going to stand; this is what we're going to do"—and in Timothy's case, his mother got her fuel from the sacred writings. Her convictions cemented Timothy to Scripture.

To a large extent, we are who we are today because of the influence of the women God placed in our lives as children. Even those of us who have lost our godly mothers still live in the lingering legacy of their lives. May their counsel never go away. May their tenderness and convictions stay with us all our years. May we, like Eunice and Lois, pass to the next generation our love for God's Word and the willingness to obey it.

—Charles R. Swindoll

The Rest of the Story: Read about the young man Eunice and Lois influenced in the letters of 1 and 2 Timothy.

Take It to *Heart*

Be an influence where you are. Whether you are a parent or not, children are watching you—at home, at church, and in your neighborhood. What are they learning? How are your responses and reactions to life reflective of your faith in Christ? Consider here what you hope your life teaches.

How to Begin a Relationship with God

If you've stood in line at a grocery store recently, you've seen for yourself the tons of messages that bombard people—and especially women—about what it means to really live. Usually focused on appearance and social status, the messages these magazines and tabloids shout offer nothing helpful to the woman who wants to know what real life is and how she can have it. Where can you go to get the truth?

This book has described women from the Bible. Some of these women knew real life and now serve as witnesses to the truth and as models of godly character in process. Some of these women rejected real life and now serve as tragic examples of where that decision leads.

People can be divided into those two simple categories: those who know life eternal and those who do not. If you hear that and wonder which group you are in, the good news is that you can know for sure.

What follows is an explanation of four truths that walk through what you need to know about eternal life—why people need it, why God qualifies to give it, how He provides it, and what you need to do to get it. The decision is yours.

Let's look at each truth one by one:

Our Spiritual Condition: Totally Depraved

The first truth is rather personal. One look in the mirror of Scripture, and our human condition becomes painfully clear:

> "There is none righteous, not even one;
> There is none who understands,
> There is none who seeks for God;
> All have turned aside, together they have
> become useless;
> There is none who does good,
> There is not even one." (Romans 3:10–12)

We are all sinners through and through—totally depraved. Now, that doesn't mean we've committed every atrocity known to humankind. We're not as *bad* as we can be, just as *bad off* as we can be. Sin colors all our thoughts, motives, words, and actions.

If you've been around a while, you likely already believe it. Look around. Everything around us bears the smudge marks of our sinful nature. Despite our best efforts to create a perfect world, crime statistics continue to soar, divorce rates keep climbing, and families keep crumbling.

Something has gone terribly wrong in our society and in ourselves—something deadly. Contrary to how the world would repackage it, "me-first" living doesn't equal rugged individuality and freedom; it equals death. As Paul said in his letter to the Romans, "The wages of sin is death" (Romans 6:23)—our spiritual and physical death that comes from God's righteous judgment of our sin, along with all of the emotional and practical effects of this separation that we experience on a daily basis. This brings us to the second marker: God's character.

God's Character: Infinitely Holy

How can God judge us for a sinful state we were born into? Our total depravity is only half the answer. The other half is God's infinite holiness.

The fact that we know things are not as they should be points us to a standard of goodness beyond ourselves. Our sense of injustice in life on this side of eternity implies a perfect standard of justice beyond our reality. That standard and source is God Himself. And God's standard of holiness contrasts starkly with our sinful condition.

Scripture says that "God is Light, and in Him there is no darkness at all" (1 John 1:5). God is absolutely holy—which creates a problem for us. If He is so pure, how can we who are so impure relate to Him?

Perhaps we could try being better people, try to tilt the balance in favor of our good deeds, or seek out methods for self-improvement. Throughout history, people have attempted to live up to God's standard by keeping the Ten Commandments or living by their own code of ethics. Unfortunately, no one can come close to satisfying the demands of God's law. Romans 3:20 says, "By the works of the Law no flesh will be justified in His sight; for through the Law comes the knowledge of sin."

Our Need: A Substitute

So here we are, sinners by nature and sinners by choice, trying to pull ourselves up by our own bootstraps to attain a relationship with our holy Creator. But every time we try, we fall flat on our faces. We can't live a good enough life to make up for our sin, because God's standard isn't "good enough"—it's *perfection*. And we can't make amends for the offense our sin has created without dying for it.

Who can get us out of this mess?

If someone could live perfectly, honoring God's law, and would bear sin's death penalty for us—in our place—then we would be saved from our predicament. But is there such a person? Thankfully, yes!

Meet your substitute—*Jesus Christ*. He is the One who took death's place for you!

> [God] made [Jesus Christ] who knew no sin to be sin on our behalf, so that we might become the righteousness of God in Him. (2 Corinthians 5:21)

God's Provision: A Savior

God rescued us by sending His Son, Jesus, to die on the cross for our sins (1 John 4:9–10). Jesus was fully human and fully divine (John 1:1, 18), a truth that ensures His understanding of our weaknesses, His power to forgive, and His ability to bridge the gap between God and us (Romans 5:6–11). In short, we are "justified as a gift by His grace through the redemption which is in Christ Jesus" (Romans 3:24). Two words in this verse bear further explanation: *justified* and *redemption*.

Justification is God's act of mercy, in which He declares righteous the believing sinners while we are still in our sinning state. Justification doesn't mean that God *makes* us righteous, so that we never sin again, rather that He *declares* us righteous—much like a judge pardons a guilty criminal. Because Jesus took our sin upon Himself and suffered our judgment on the cross, God forgives our debt and proclaims us PARDONED.

Redemption is Christ's act of paying the complete price to release us from sin's bondage. God sent His Son to bear His wrath for all of our sins—past, present, and future (Romans 3:24–26; 2 Corinthians 5:21). In humble obedience, Christ willingly endured the shame of the cross for our sake (Mark 10:45; Romans 5:6–8; Philippians 2:8). Christ's death satisfied God's righteous demands. He no longer holds our sins against us, because His own Son paid the penalty for them. We are freed from the slave market of sin, never to be enslaved again!

Placing Your Faith in Christ

These four truths describe how God has provided a way to Himself through Jesus Christ. Because the price has been paid in full by God, we must respond to His free gift of eternal life in total faith and confidence in Him to save us. We must step forward into the relationship with God that He has prepared for us—not by doing good works or by being a good person, but by coming to Him just as we are and accepting His justification and redemption by faith.

For by grace you have been saved through faith; and that not of yourselves, it is the gift of God; not as a result of works, so that no one may boast. (Ephesians 2:8–9)

We accept God's gift of salvation simply by placing our faith in Christ alone for the forgiveness of our sins. Would you like to enter a relationship with your Creator by trusting in Christ as your Savior? If so, here's a simple prayer you can use to express your faith:

> *Dear God,*
>
> *I know that my sin has put a barrier between You and me. Thank You for sending Your Son, Jesus, to die in my place. I trust in Jesus alone to forgive my sins, and I accept His gift of eternal life. I ask Jesus to be my personal Savior and the Lord of my life. Thank You. In Jesus's name, amen.*

If you've prayed this prayer or one like it and you wish to find out more about knowing God and His plan for you in the Bible, contact us at Insight for Living. Our contact information is on the following pages.

We Are Here for You

If you desire to find out more about knowing God and His plan for you in the Bible, contact us. Insight for Living provides staff pastors who are available for free written correspondence or phone consultation. These seminary-trained and seasoned counselors have years of experience and are well-qualified guides for your spiritual journey.

Please feel welcome to contact your regional Pastoral Ministries by using the information below:

United States

Insight for Living
Pastoral Ministries
Post Office Box 269000
Plano, Texas 75026-9000
USA
972-473-5097, Monday through Friday,
8:00 a.m.–5:00 p.m. Central time
www.insight.org/contactapastor

Canada

Insight for Living Canada
Pastoral Ministries
Post Office Box 2510
Vancouver, BC V6B 3W7
CANADA
1-800-663-7639
info@insightforliving.ca

Australia, New Zealand, and South Pacific

Insight for Living Australia
Pastoral Care
Post Office Box 443
Boronia, VIC 3155
AUSTRALIA
1 300 467 444

United Kingdom and Europe

Insight for Living United Kingdom
Pastoral Care
PO Box 553
Dorking
RH4 9EU
UNITED KINGDOM
0800 915 9364
+44 (0)1306 640156
pastoralcare@insightforliving.org.uk

Resources for Probing Further

Bookstores, online sites, and grocery store checkout lines are literally flooded with reading options for the modern woman. No one is shy about offering an opinion regarding how a woman should think, feel, prioritize, and live. A godly woman must choose wisely which of these clamoring voices gets her attention. We are grateful that you've trusted Insight for Living with your interest in this small volume. If you'd like to read more about the women of the Bible, we recommend the resources below. Of course, we cannot always endorse everything a writer or ministry says, so we encourage you to approach these and all other non-biblical resources with discernment.

> Incline your ear and hear the words of the
>   wise,
> And apply your mind to my knowledge;
> For it will be pleasant if you keep them
>   within you,
> That they may be ready on your lips.
> So that your trust may be in the LORD.
>   (Proverbs 22:17–19)

George, Elizabeth. *The Remarkable Women of the Bible: And Their Message for Your Life Today*. Eugene, Ore.: Harvest House, 2003.

Insight for Living. *Character Counts: Building a Life That Pleases God Bible Companion*. Plano, Tex.: Insight for Living, 2008.

Insight for Living, *Insight's Bible Companion for Women*, Vol. 3. Plano, Tex.: Insight for Living, 2001.

Insight for Living. *Releasing Worry and Finding Worth as a Woman. LifeMaps*. Plano, Tex: Insight for Living, 2009.

Lockyer, Herbert. *All the Women of the Bible*. Grand Rapids: Zondervan, 1988.

MacArthur, John. *Twelve Extraordinary Women: How God Shaped Women of the Bible and What He Wants to Do with You*. Nashville: Thomas Nelson, 2005.

Swindoll, Charles R. *Esther: A Woman of Strength and Dignity*. Great Lives Series. Nashville: W Publishing, 1997.

Swindoll, Charles R. *Fascinating Stories of Forgotten Lives*. Great Lives Series. Nashville: W Publishing, 2005.

Swindoll, Charles R. *Life Lessons Just for Women*. CD series. Plano, Tex.: Insight for Living, 2008.

Swindoll, Charles R. *Mother's Day 2008: The Lingering Legacy of a Godly Mother*. CD message. Plano, Tex.: Insight for Living, 2008.

Ordering Information

If you would like to order additional copies of *The Wise and the Wild: 30 Devotions on Women of the Bible* or order other Insight for Living resources, please contact the office that serves you.

United States

Insight for Living
Post Office Box 269000
Plano, Texas 75026-9000
USA
1-800-772-8888
Monday through Friday
7:00 a.m. – 7:00 p.m. Central time
www.insight.org
www.insightworld.org

Canada

Insight for Living Canada
Post Office Box 2510
Vancouver, BC V6B 3W7
CANADA
1-800-663-7639
www.insightforliving.ca

Australia, New Zealand, and South Pacific

Insight for Living Australia
Post Office Box 443
Boronia, VIC 3155
AUSTRALIA
1 300 467 444
www.insight.asn.au

United Kingdom and Europe

Insight for Living United Kingdom
PO Box 553
Dorking
RH4 9EU
UNITED KINGDOM
0800 915 9364
www.insightforliving.org.uk

Other International Locations

International constituents may contact the U.S. office through our Web site (www.insightworld.org), mail queries, or by calling +1-972-473-5136.

About the Writers

Charles R. Swindoll

Chancellor of Dallas Theological Seminary and best-selling author, Chuck Swindoll also serves as senior pastor of Stonebriar Community Church in Frisco, Texas, where he's able to do what he loves most — teach the Bible to willing hearts. His focus on practical Bible application has been heard on the *Insight for Living* radio broadcast since 1979.

John Adair

John has been married to Laura for more than fifteen years. They have three children and currently make their home in Frisco, Texas. John received his Ph.D. in historical theology from Dallas Theological Seminary, and he now serves as a writer in Creative Ministries of Insight for Living.

Derrick G. Jeter

Strong-willed and wise women have always been a part of Derrick's life. Growing up as the only boy among two sisters and living near two grandmothers with forceful personalities, Derrick learned early on to respect the wisdom of women.

Now, after more than twenty years of marriage to Christy and raising five children, one of whom is a teenage daughter, he has learned to admire a woman's wisdom. Derrick is a graduate of Dallas Theological Seminary and serves as a writer for Insight for Living.

Barb Peil

As one of the first women to graduate from Dallas Theological Seminary, Barb knows what it's like to be a woman in a man's world. But it doesn't scare her. Far from it; she counts herself especially blessed to have enjoyed a couple of decades (so far) in ministry in the world of education, writing, and Christian radio. Barb received her master of arts in Christian Education from Dallas Theological Seminary and serves as managing editor and assistant writer at Insight for Living.

Wayne Stiles

Wayne is first and foremost a husband to Cathy and a daddy to their two teenage daughters. After serving in the pastorate for fourteen years, Wayne joined the staff of Insight for Living and currently serves as executive vice president and chief content officer. He received his master of theology and doctor of ministry degrees from Dallas Theological Seminary.